GREAT AMERICAN
HORSES
AN IMAGINATION LIBRARY SERIES

CHINCOTEAGUE
PONIES

by Victor Gentle and Janet Perry

Gareth Stevens Publishing
A WORLD ALMANAC EDUCATION GROUP COMPANY

This book would not exist were it not for the passion and dedication of
Kendy Allen for her Chincoteague Pony herd, her Drill Team, and Misty II.
—Victor Gentle and Janet Perry

Please visit our web site at: www.garethstevens.com
For a free color catalog describing Gareth Stevens' list of high-quality books and
multimedia programs, call 1-800-542-2595 (USA) or 1-800-461-9120 (Canada).
Gareth Stevens Publishing's Fax: (414) 332-3567.

Library of Congress Cataloging-in-Publication Data

Gentle, Victor.
   Chincoteague ponies / by Victor Gentle and Janet Perry.
      p. cm. — (Great American horses: an imagination library series)
   Includes bibliographical references (p. 23) and index.
   ISBN 0-8368-2935-2 (lib. bdg.)
   1. Chincoteague pony—Assateague Island (Md. and Va.)—Juvenile literature.
[1. Chincoteague pony. 2. Ponies. 3. Horses.] I. Perry, Janet, 1960- II. Title.
SF315.2.C4G46   2001
636.1'6—dc21   2001020851

First published in 2001 by
Gareth Stevens Publishing
A World Almanac Education Group Company
330 West Olive Street, Suite 100
Milwaukee, WI 53212 USA

Text: Victor Gentle and Janet Perry
Page layout: Victor Gentle, Janet Perry, and Scott M. Krall
Cover design: Renee M. Bach
Series editor: Katherine J. Meitner
Picture researcher: Diane Laska-Swanke

Photo credits: Cover © K. B. Sandved/Visuals Unlimited; pp. 5, 13, 22 © Bob Langrish; pp. 7 (main), 9
© Medford Taylor/NGS Image Collection; p. 7 (inset) Scott M. Krall/© Gareth Stevens, Inc., 2001; p. 11
© Beth Davidow/Visuals Unlimited; p. 15 Courtesy of Peter Stone, Misty of Chincoteague Foundation; p. 17
Courtesy of Don Dostie; pp. 19, 21 Courtesy of Kendy Allen and the Chincoteague Pony Drill Team

Printed in the United States of America

1 2 3 4 5 6 7 8 9 05 04 03 02 01

Front cover: A Chincoteague Pony **mare** and her colt
eat at the edge of a salt marsh. A lifetime of chewing
salt-filled grasses wears down the ponies' teeth.

TABLE OF CONTENTS

Words that appear in the glossary are printed in **boldface** type the first time they occur in the text.

MAROONED!

How the Chincoteague (SHIN-ko-teeg) Ponies got to Assateague Island is a mystery. Wild tales are told that are as thick as the fogs that settle on the island itself.

Was this little herd trapped when the last ice age swept through North America? Were they castaways from Spanish shipwrecks? Did pirates steal them and leave them on the island? Or did European colonists hide them in this place, like a secret treasure, hoping thieves wouldn't find them?

"All I know is, when my great-great-great-grandfather got over here, those ponies had been there for a while," says Richard Conklin, director of the Chincoteague Pony Centre.

However Chincoteague Ponies got to Assateague Island, they came in many colors and patterns. They can be red, gray, and spotted.

TWO OF A KIND

If the ponies live on Assateague Island, why are they called Chincoteague Ponies? Each year, some of the ponies swim from Assateague Island to Chincoteague Island. The **breed** is named after Chincoteague, where they are sold at auction.

There are two herds — the Maryland herd and the Virginia herd. They both live on Assateague and are separated by a fence. The Maryland herd lives in a national park. The Chincoteague Volunteer Fire Company owns the Virginia herd.

The Maryland herd is left alone, but the firefighters visit the Virginia herd three times a year. They have a veterinarian check the ponies if they are hurt or sick and feed them during rough winters.

If any Chincoteague Ponies cannot make the swim, the firefighters cart them to and from Chincoteague Island in trailers. Inset: A map of Chincoteague.

MARYLAND

VIRGINIA

CHINCOTEAGUE
ISLAND

ASSATEAGUE
ISLAND

PONY PENNING DAY!

The firefighters and the Virginia ponies have a special relationship. By law, the Virginia herd cannot have more than 150 ponies. New **foals** are born every year, which raises the number of ponies on Assateague Island.

Since there are extra ponies and the Fire Company needs money, each year the firefighters hold a carnival and a "Pony Penning" auction. They round up the ponies and swim them to Chincoteague. After a day's rest, they sell some of the foals and yearlings. The next day, any ponies that were not sold swim back to Assateague, where they are free once more.

A firefighter ropes young ponies for auction. The auction began in the 1920s, when the Fire Company needed equipment.

MADE OF TOUGH STUFF

Chincoteague Ponies are small, but sturdy. They have to be. Assateague Island is a hard place to live. Since Assateague is a **barrier island**, the coastal storms, winds, and waves lash there first. The scruffy little trees on the island provide poor shelter in storms and hardly any shade in the hot sun. For the most part, the ponies tough it out in the open.

Saltgrass, cordgrass, twigs, and berries are all that Chincoteague Ponies have to eat. **Brackish water**, which is salty, is all they have to drink. To get the nutrition they need from this poor food and water, they eat and drink lots and lots. So they are not chubby, just really full of food and water!

This pony looks a little fat. Actually, it is just extra full of saltwater, bark, and grass stems.

BORN TO BE WILD?

Did Chincoteague Ponies get tough because they live on Assateague? Or were they just born with the right stuff? Probably both. Life on Assateague no doubt made them tougher, but they had to have the right qualities to survive in the first place.

Their ancestors were probably fine, durable Spanish horses and strong British work ponies since Chincoteague Ponies have fine bones like Spanish horses and muscular bodies like British work ponies. Some are **pintos**, with showy patches of color. Others have solid colors like brown, black, or gray.

Like most ponies, Chincoteagues get very shaggy in cold weather, can get by on the poorest food, and are 14 **hands** high or less, although a few are taller.

Chincoteague Ponies now have a breed registry — a kind of family record. They must have parents that are both Chincoteague Ponies.

A FOAL THE WORLD WOULD LOVE

In 1946, a woman named Marguerite Henry went to Pony Penning Day and her life was changed forever. She bought a yellow and white spotted Chincoteague Pony foal from a man called Grandpa Beebe. He told her to wait until the foal grew big enough to travel all the way to her home in Illinois. Ms. Henry named the **filly** Misty.

Soon after Misty moved into her new home, she made many friends. Neighbor kids loved to visit Misty. Then came Friday the Morgan horse, Momcat and her kittens, and a burro named Jiggs.

Ms. Henry wrote two great stories that made Misty world famous: *Misty of Chincoteague* and *Stormy, Misty's Foal*.

Here are Misty and Ms. Henry at Mole Meadow stable in Wayne, Illinois. Misty's books were also made into a movie, called *Misty of Chincoteague*.

SWEET AND SHOWY

Because of Misty's famous life story, many people learned about Chincoteague Ponies. Like Misty, most Chincoteague Ponies are sweet, gentle, and very smart.

In 1994, a Chincoteague Pony named Nick moved to Chincoteague Island and became a barnyard buddy to lots of kids that live nearby. The children love to visit, feed, and groom him. They also give Nick as many hugs as they can. He is a terrific pet!

Chincoteague Ponies make great friends. Since ponies and horses are friendly, training them is easy when they want to please you. That is why great pony friends also make outstanding show ponies.

Nick gets a hug from one of his many friends.

FRIENDS AND PARTNERS

Chincoteague Ponies have been trained in equitation, **dressage**, jumping, pole racing, barrel racing, and drill team work.

Equitation is a competition where riders and ponies are judged on how well they work together while the pony walks, **trots**, **lopes**, and **canters**. In dressage competitions, ponies are taught to do a precise series of movements. In the racing events, riders gallop their ponies as fast as they can around poles or barrels.

A drill team is a group of horses and riders that performs a pattern of movements to music, just like dancers or marching bands. It takes a lot of practice, but everyone has a good time!

Chincoteague Ponies are talented in all fields! Top left: Practicing for a show. Top right: Jumping. Bottom left: Winning ribbons. Bottom right: Resting in the shade.

WINNING WAYS

Today, there is only one Chincoteague Pony Drill Team in the world. The riders are anywhere from eight to twenty years old. In 2000, the team competed at a festival called Equitana against slick-looking teams with well-matched horses.

When they practiced in the new ring, things went badly. Then, on the day of competition, the wrong music played! As team captain Kerra Allen says, "We pulled together and did the drills better than we ever had!" They got a standing ovation and became Youth Exhibition Champions.

The plucky ponies from Assateague are all-around winners — in the struggle to survive, in horse show competitions, and in our hearts.

It's a Drill Team salute! Like their riders, each pony is different. Their hair color and sizes might not match, but together, they are winners.

DIAGRAM AND SCALE OF A HORSE

Here's how to measure a horse with a show of hands.
This **stallion** is marked by bright eyes and clean movement.

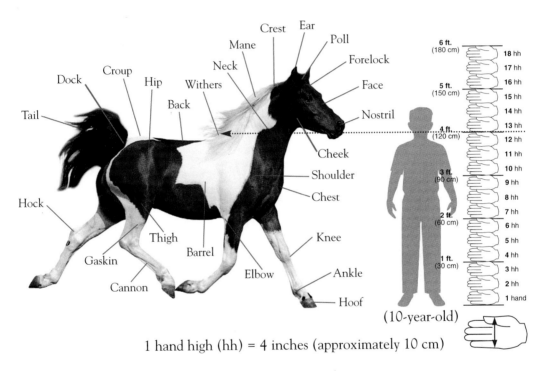

1 hand high (hh) = 4 inches (approximately 10 cm)

WHERE TO WRITE OR CALL FOR MORE INFORMATION

Chincoteague Pony Association
P.O. Box 691
Chincoteague Island, VA 23336
Phone: (757) 336-6917

22

MORE TO READ AND VIEW

Books (Fiction):   *Misty of Chincoteague*. Marguerite Henry (Aladdin)
Sea Feather. Lois Szymanski (Avon)
Sea Star: Orphan of Chincoteague. Marguerite Henry (Aladdin)
Stormy, Misty's Foal. Marguerite Henry (Aladdin)

Books (Nonfiction):   *Assateague: Island of Wild Ponies*. Larry Points
(Panorama International Products)
The Complete Guides to Horses and Ponies (series). Jackie Budd
(Gareth Stevens)
*The United States Pony Club Manual of Horsemanship: Basics for
Beginners*. Susan E. Harris (Hungry Minds)

Magazines: *Horse Illustrated* and its magazine for young readers, *Young Rider*

Videos (Fiction):   *Misty of Chincoteague Island*. (Columbia River)

Videos (Nonfiction):   *Noble Horse*. (National Geographic)
Ultimate Guide to Horses. (Discovery Channel)

WEB SITES

Chincoteague Pony Centre
www.chincoteague.com/ponycentre

For general horse information:
www.imh.org/imh/imhmain.html

For more about Chincoteague Ponies:
www.nickie.net/DrillTeam.html
www.mistyofchincoteague.org
www.pony-chincoteague.com

Some web sites stay current longer than others. To find additional web sites, use a reliable search engine, such as Yahooligans or KidsClick! (http://sunsite.berkeley.edu/KidsClick!/), with one or more of the following key words to help you locate information about horses: *Assateague Island*, *Chincoteague Ponies*, *dressage*, *equitation*, and *ranch*.

GLOSSARY

You can find these words on the pages listed. Reading a word in a sentence helps you understand it even better.

barrier island — an island, usually long and narrow, that partially protects a mainland coast from the weather 6

brackish water — mildly salty water 10

breed (n) — a group of horses that shares the same features as a result of careful selection of stallions and mares to produce foals 6, 12

canter (KANT-ur) — to run with a gait that has a complicated three-beat style 18

dressage (druh-SAHJ) — training a horse to perform gaits in an orderly way 18

filly — a female horse, less than four years old 14

foal (FOHL) — a young horse that is less than one year old 8, 14

hand — a unit used to measure horses. It is equal to 4 inches (10.2 cm), about the width of a human hand 12, 22

lope — to run in a relaxed manner 18

mare — an adult female horse 2

pinto (PIN-toe) — a horse with large patches of color 12

stallion — an adult male horse 22

trot — to run with a gait that has two beats, where diagonally opposite legs hit the ground at the same time 18

INDEX